TO

_____

FROM

_____

*Hope is the best part
of our riches.*

CHRISTIAN NESTELL BOVEE

The GIFT *of*
small comforts

HOPE LYDA

KPT|PUBLISHING

The Gift of Small Comforts
Copyright © 2017 Written and compiled by Hope Lyda

Published by KPT Publishing
Minneapolis, Minnesota 55406
www.KPTPublishing.com

ISBN 978-1-944833-17-6

Design and production by Koechel Peterson and Associates, Minneapolis, Minnesota

All rights reserved. No part of this publication may be reproduced, stored in a retrieval system, or transmitted in any form or by any means—electronic, mechanical, digital, photocopy, recording, or any other—except for brief quotations in printed reviews, without the prior permission of the publishers.

First printing March 2017

10 9 8 7 6 5 4 3 2 1

Printed in the United States of America

A multitude of small delights constitute happiness.

CHARLES BAUDELAIRE

What is your life like today?

did a change in plans create a steady stream of worries?

has a loss left you with a fragile heart?

Whatever you face,

THIS PLACE IS YOUR SHELTER.

Your home.

Your refuge.

This sliver of space expands to cover

your every need. This is the magic of the heart's sanctuary.

Where we love is home,
home that our feet may leave,
but not our hearts.

OLIVER WENDELL HOLMES

When was the last time you said, *"Ahhh"*...

and *really* meant it.

Be glad of life, because it gives you
the chance to live and to work and
to play and to look up at the stars.

HENRY VAN DYKE

Shed your burdens and settle in.

This gathering of small comforts

is just for you.

Dive in or savor them one by one...

whatever makes you comfortable

is just right.

Cure sometimes, treat often,

comfort always.

HIPPOCRATES

Your senses are your connection

to life's abundant simple pleasures. Rest in this for today.

Survey the wonders that bring a smile to your lips,

an ease to your breath, a momentum to your step.

These are the gifts you can draw from

ANYTIME, ANYWHERE.

*Nothing can cure the soul but the senses, just
as nothing can cure the senses but the soul.*

OSCAR WILDE

Look around for signs of hope and life.
The rosy cheeks of a baby. The first
brave bud of spring. A hawk soaring
across a summer sky. Whatever sparks
joy, recall such images...

and set out today with the intention to witness

new sights of awe with gratitude.

I try to avoid looking forward
or backward, and try to
keep looking upward.

CHARLOTTE BRONTË

Is it so small a thing
To have enjoy'd the sun,
To have lived in the spring,
To have loved, to have thought,
to have done?

MATTHEW ARNOLD

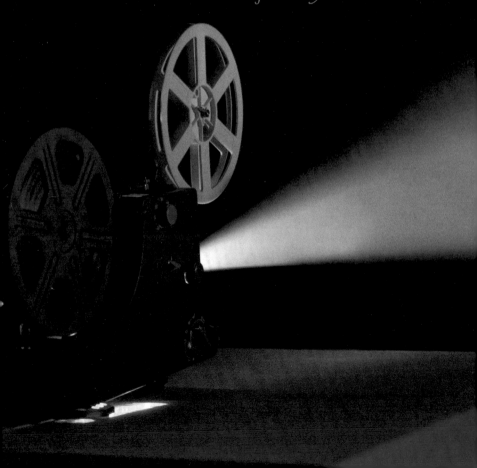

*Watch an **old movie** that reframes your outlook…*

Relish that delightful moment
of anticipation when the lights
go down and a new story begins.
Envision your new story.

(SPOILER ALERT: *It's a good one.*)

*One's destination is never a place but
rather a new way of looking at things.*

HENRY MILLER

Pay attention to the kaleidoscope

of beauty around you...

journey through life. Deliver a visual bouquet to your soul: a red bike with happy blue streamers, a field of white daisies, a ring of turquoise. Take the time to gather images that *splash wonder across your imagination.*

Happiness is not a state to arrive at,
but a manner of traveling.

MARGARET LEE RUNBECK

Far away there in the sunshine
  are my highest aspirations.
  I may not reach them, but I can look up
and see their beauty, believe in them,
  and try to follow where they lead.

LOUISA MAY ALCOTT

Spend a measure of eternity *gazing* at the stars...

The vast night sky is a playground for your imagination and your every hope. Make a wish right now that brightens your view of tomorrow.

Light tomorrow with today.

ELIZABETH BARRETT BROWNING

Grand gestures get the fanfare,

but it is the small joys, tender graces,

and simple pleasures that transform a life.

Trust this each time you are touched
BY AN ACT OF KINDNESS,

an offer of help,

or a soothing daily ritual.

These comforts are extended to you

without limit, without strings.

The wealth of man is the number
of things which he loves and blesses,
which he is loved and blessed by.

THOMAS CARLYLE

Life is made up, not of great sacrifices or duties,
but of little things, in which smiles, and kindnesses,
and small obligations, given habitually, are what
win and preserve the heart and secure comfort.

SIR H. DAVY

How long has it been since you
stood barefoot on the lawn
or felt sand massage your soles?

Celebrate your next step.

It will be taken on sacred ground.

The foolish man seeks happiness in the distance;

the wise grows it under his feet.

JAMES OPPENHEIM

Feel relief cover you as a friend

reaches for your hand. . .

Remember, we all stumble, every one of us.
That's why it's a comfort to go hand-in-hand.

EMILY KIMBROUGH

and offers words of assurance. *You can do this.*
I think you're amazing. Lean on me when you are weary.
It's so much easier to press on when
someone dear walks beside you;
when someone lifts you up.

Write your name in kindness,
    love, and mercy on the hearts of thousands
        you come in contact with year by year,
and you will never be forgotten.
        Your name and your good deeds
            will shine as the stars of heaven.

THOMAS CHALMERS

Hold a smooth, white rock in your hand.

Turn it round and round to warm your

palm. Let the weight of nature's

sculpture be your sure comfort.

You, too, are a work of creation's art.

To see a World in a Grain of Sand,
    And a Heaven in a Wild Flower,
Hold Infinity in the palm of your hand,
    An Eternity in an hour.

WILLIAM BLAKE

Shush the no. Silence the clamoring shoulds.

Recline in the stillness with your feet perched on a giant down pillow

and your head grazing the clouds. Suspend your need to

wrap up details

or tie up loose ends.

DREAM UP

something splendid instead!

Besides the noble art of getting
things done, there is a nobler
art of leaving things undone.

LIN YUTANG

When you feel lost in the chaos

or the heartache, remember that you are not alone.

You are...noticed, nourished, beloved, and lifted up.

Listen for messages of this

SUPPORT AND CARE.

They are being whispered to you beneath the
white noise of a demanding day.

Be inspired with the belief that life is a great
and noble calling; not a mean and groveling
thing that we are to shuffle through as we can,
but an elevated and lofty destiny.

WILLIAM E. GLADSTONE

To listen to stars and birds,

babes and sages, **with open heart;**

to study hard; to think quietly, act frankly, talk

gently, await occasions, hurry never; in a word,

to let the spiritual, unbidden and unconscious,

grow up through the common—this is my symphony.

WILLIAM HENRY CHANNING

The world is serenading you with a song of vitality and motivation. Turn it up. Sway to the melody. Cha Cha with courageous abandon. Tap those toes. *No rhythm is required—this is the soundtrack of destiny and grace.*

My idea is that there is music in the air,
music all around us; the world is
full of it, and you simply take
as much as you require.

EDWARD ELGAR

If life is centered on trials right now, create the space to be off-center. Your assignment is to listen to the sound of your own LAUGHTER. So chuckle. Chortle. Guffaw for extra credit!

Call the relative whose crazy antics and tall tales make you giggle. Set aside time for the important task of play. Finger paint, juggle, or spend an afternoon with your pet pal. Recall what made your best friend spit out her chocolate milk in the grade school cafeteria.

(ANSWER: *She was laughing.*)

The most wasted of all days is that in which we have not laughed.

NICOLAS CHAMFORT

The place to be happy is here.
The time to be happy is now.
The way to be happy is to make others so.

Robert Ingersoll

With the new day comes new strength and new thoughts.

ELEANOR ROOSEVELT

When was the last time
  you had a heart-to-heart...

with a dear friend? A loved one? Make that call.

Even if you are rusty, cold silences will melt into connection and

gratitude. If your special person is no longer here, speak aloud to them.

Tell them about your life and what you
loved most about being in their presence.

WORDS SPOKEN FROM THE SOUL

always get to where they need to go.

Let us be grateful to people who make us
happy, they are the charming gardeners
who make our souls blossom.

MARCEL PROUST

There are two ways of spreading light: to be the candle or the mirror that reflects it.

EDITH WHARTON

Hope, like the gleaming taper's light,
Adorns and cheers our way.

OLIVER GOLDSMITH

Surrender to the intoxicating scent of the sea.

Relish the zing of salt on your tongue.

Pucker up at the sight of a dazzling lemon.

Breathe in the perfume of a garden at dusk.

An unlimited buffet of fragrances

and flavors is laid out before you.

Take time to savor your bit of bliss today.

I go to nature to be soothed
and healed, and to have
my senses put in order.

JOHN BURROUGHS

This is just a taste of what you deserve...

A BAKER'S DOZEN OF YOUR FAVORITE DECADENT TREATS.

Joy that inspires possibility.

Praises for your extraordinary ways.

A year filled with surprises that knock your socks off.

(Then a pair of velvet slippers so your toes stay warm.)

If you haven't received these treasures, be sure to give them to yourself.

Life is short, and it's up to you to make it sweet.

SARAH LOUISE DELANEY

Happiness resides not in
possessions and not in gold;
*the feeling of happiness
dwells in the soul.*

DEMOCRITUS

*This day calls for extra helpings
of your favorite comfort food.*

What will it be? A grilled cheese sandwich paired with creamy

tomato soup? Crispy fried chicken and mashed potatoes?

Oh, what about homemade biscuits and gravy? Peach cobbler

with vanilla ice cream? Or maybe those sweet

blueberry scones your grandma used to serve with tea?

While your palate is being pleased,

dine on memories that fill

YOU UP WITH JOY AND

SATE YOUR SOUL.

Pour away despair and rinse the cup.
Eat happiness like bread.

EDNA ST. VINCENT MILLAY

If this season of life isn't what you bargained for,

resist the urge to scramble to find the cause.

Feed your spirit with stillness. Nourish the hunger for peace.

BREATHE DEEPLY.

Exhale worries and what-ifs...

Inhale goodness and gratitude.

Best of all is it to preserve everything in a pure,
still heart, and let there be for every pulse a
thanksgiving, and for every breath a song.

CONRAD GESSNER

Listen to your life. See it for the fathomless mystery that it is. In the boredom and pain of it no less than the excitement and gladness: touch, taste, smell your way to the holy and hidden heart of it, because in the last analysis all moments are key moments, and life itself is grace.

FREDERICK BUECHNER